I0499785

This book belongs to:

____